PHYSICAL

PHYSICAL

Andrew McMillan

CAPE POETRY

Published by Jonathan Cape 2015

2 4 6 8 10 9 7 5 3

First published in Great Britain in 2015 by
Jonathan Cape
Random House, 20 Vauxhall Bridge Road,
London SW1V 2SA

www.randomhouse.co.uk

Addresses for companies within The Random House Group Limited can be found at
www.randomhouse.co.uk/offices.htm

The Random House Group Limited Reg. No. 954009

A CIP catalogue record for this book
is available from the British Library

ISBN 9780224102131

Penguin Random House is committed to a sustainable future for
our business, our readers and our planet. This book is made from
Forest Stewardship Council® certified paper

Typeset by Palimpsest Book Production Ltd, Falkirk, Stirlingshire
Printed and bound in Great Britain by
TJ International Ltd, Cornwall

for my parents

CONTENTS

i

physical

You are trembling.

It's the way I crooked my elbow, you know, this way
— it's nothing —

H.D., *Bid Me to Live*

JACOB WITH THE ANGEL

taken literally   it just happens   the way the weather
or the stock market   *happens*
tangling in the unpierced flesh of one another
grappling with the shifting question of each other's bodies
until the morning breaks across them and still their strength
no soft parts of stomachs   no inch of them hung loose
like old sacking from the muscle
and burning afterwards   or barely able to walk afterwards
or not giving a name because names would add a history
and the tasting of the flesh and blood of someone
is something out of time

taken allegorically   he is beating on himself
until the point at which the inner river of the word *grace*
runs past and everything lays down in calm
and walking back across the stream to his possessions
he feels the bruise that is staining his thigh
and he wonders at the strength of one so smooth
and his wives and womenservants and his sons
are sat waiting for the story
but he sleeps without speaking and on waking
isn't sure if he has dreamt it
but his youngest notices the thresh marks of wingbeats
on his back and he asks for ink to be brought
he says writing something down   keeps it alive

URINATION

I'm scared of bumping someone while they piss
those Mondays I'm a packhorse   bags hung
swinging around the urinal bodies
and one day   I know   I'll knock someone
and they'll piss their legs   or they'll turn slightly
and show another man their full arc
or they'll fall into their own wet puddle
cock limp   and neither of us will look
or he'll look at me avoiding looking
feigning interest in the hard cream tiles
maybe it's that I dream of being bumped
knocked from my aim by a stranger
the briefest touch during the private act
the toilet is an intimacy
only shared with parents when you are young
and once again when they are older
and with lovers when   say   on a Sunday
morning stretching into the bathroom
you wake to the sound of stream into bowl
and go to hug the naked body
stood with its back to you   and kiss the neck
and taste the whole of the night on there
and smell the morning's pale yellow loss
and take the whole of him in your hand
and feel the water moving through him
and knowing that this is love   the prone flesh
what we expel from the body and what we let inside

THE MEN ARE WEEPING IN THE GYM

the men are weeping in the gym
using the hand dryer to cover
their sobs   their hearts have grown too big
for their chests   their chests have grown too big
for their shirts   they are dressed like kids
who have forgotten their games kit
they are crying in the toilet
and because they have built themselves
as statues this must mean that God
has entered them   they are wringing
their faces like sweat towels
in the sink   their veins are about
to burst their banks   they are flooding
out of themselves onto the tiles
they have turned water into protein shakes
they have got too close to the mirrors
they have got too close to the glass
and now they are laying
in the broken pools of their own faces
the lines of them!   at the decline press
the bicep curl   waiting   staring
straight ahead   swearing that the wetness
on their cheeks is perspiration
that the words they mutter as they lift
are meaningless   that they feel
nothing when the muscle tears itself
from itself   that they don't hear
the thousands of tiny fracturings
needed to build something stronger

STRONGMAN

my nephew asks if I can benchpress him
his mother's new lover can and often does

my nephew who once said my boyfriend was illegal
my nephew with his dad's voice and jaw

my nephew who now protests I had my hand
on his balls for the first attempt

I try again   let both his wicket legs
rest against one palm   put my other

to his heart   and push   because
what is masculinity if not taking the weight

of a boy and straining it from oneself?
here we are   a man holding a boy above him

horizontal   like an offering to the artex ceiling
not even a minor Greek would see as fit to sculpt

YOGA

we are told to tell our bodies that they are beautiful
we are told not to pass judgement
on where the breath may fall
in the dry heat of July we bend our bodies beyond
their normal boundaries   push past the bones until we look
like unkempt foliage   delirious in our own abandon
we are told to root our feet into the ground   we are told
to hear all sounds around us as vibrations   we have
forgotten that the body can hold on to negativity
we are told to sigh this out   we are told that only empty
things are light enough to fly   we end by flying   hoisting
up our partners by our feet   taking the weight
on our forearms on the ground   the flier feels bodiless
until the heft begins to shake the legs and the architecture
of the limbs collapses   it needs trust in the strengthofbody
of another to support your own   to delay
and then control the falling   later   showered   fed
and still too warm   stretched out on the mattress
in the new flat   nothing but dust on the bare walls
you pressed me down   took control
took me in your mouth   I regret now being so passive
but you made me feel weightless   and the next night
light gone in the hallway   I felt my way to you to kiss you
I had forgotten that loving could feel so calming
telling you that your body was beautiful   sighing out
the brittle disappointments from the bones
having no judgement of what the body
may want to be doing   where the breath may fall

THE SCHOOLBOYS

coming with the bulge of them through the doors
schoolboys in suits so big it seems as though
grown men have deflated inside   two slump
away from the morning rush of bags   phones
arms stretched out of their muscle by the sharp
sprints of growth   they find their seats and settle

facing me   first fluff ready for shaving
but left to go feral above the lip
words sweating into the air between them
the twelveyearold talk that finds the body
still comical rather than alluring
they briefly mention Thatcher and the town

that came together for a party   they
didn't understand the point of   although
the adults seemed to enjoy it   *drinking*
and setting fire to a doll of her
one makes a joke insult to the other
who pretends to be offended   pouting

into his rucksack then out the window
there's silence   but they are still only
learning stubbornness and buckle quickly
the insulter takes his friend's face in
one hand   pushing his thin lips together
to parody the mood   the lady sat

by the side of me tuts   the boys let go
and start their conversation up again
one puts his hand between the cheap trousers
of the other   the way schoolgirls often
hold hands on their way to class   the woman
coughs and sighs like a slowpunctured football

she stares out the window   maybe thinking
of her son   by now a man   she goes red
she focuses on a headline   *rising*
unemployment   lack of manual jobs
the boys move seats   two others wrestle
to impress the girls   the boys sit closer
than they need to   the lady burns

SCREEN

at the beginning I asked you
to let me watch you watching porn   I think
I needed to see you existing
entirely without me   your face lost

in concentration on another's
rhythm   to know if we could work   I knew
that you would end up loving me too
much   I thought you needed other idols

months later   I saw him   the actor
from that film we watched   unmissable
petals of the neck tattoo   he seemed
to look at me as though he knew I'd seen

him naked   his body a deep well
of things I would not ask a living soul
to do   I wanted to shout   *stranger*   *I*
have seen your skin and you are beautiful

he was standing at the train station
more vulnerable than I remembered
much smaller too   I imagined him
heavy with the hope of other men

taking someone home   the look on his face
when he realised how timid
he was without direction   how
ordinary the unlit curves

of his shoulders were   I imagined him
stopping mid kiss   pulling back   mumbling
this just isn't going how I wanted
this just isn't going to work

JUST BECAUSE I DO THIS, DOESN'T MEAN

not knowing names doesn't make it something less
the midroad fight over red jumper and bike
doesn't make it something more   it was just

   a long walk through see saw streets   a stomach
   stretched tight as drumskin over hollow abdomen
   mouths finding every part of one another

   watching the mirror like a laptop screen
   a moon that kept trying to light us but kept off
   a flat full of shortflightstopover

   the one who wanted to pretend he was wrestling
   to be pinned under the anxious face of the clock watching
   the kisses that wanted to stay for longer than a night

   the one who said he wanted to write
   the way an old woman in slippers
   might say she used to want to be a dancer

   the heavy scent of them as they showered and I dressed
   running until I was breathless in the centre of town
   it wasn't the rain   the rain hadn't come yet   but it would

SATURDAY NIGHT

a broken cento for Thom Gunn

bedless and hungry   the night's pull drags me
to a street it seems I only half knew
and now paid up   stripped off   and towelled
I prowl the labyrinthine corridors

and think that everything I read in Gunn
or watched in porn was true   bodies of men
line the walls and I feel the ceiling drip
and have a sense of being underground

no air that doesn't smell of someone on
the breath of someone else   and when I call
your name to slow you it comes out strangled
as in a mine   dim light   the many floors

the private cell we visit first   the man
who keeps on shouting that we shouldn't fall
asleep   then on to the TV benches
the bays   the heat   the tape's explosive sound

reminders of the club that we climbed up from
and then heard in the distance as we walked
and you said we should try this (where we could see
people still entering   though it was 3 a.m.)

and wound up here   sitting on an L shaped bench
watching a film that could have been of us   except
I lacked the guts of the two boys flashed up to us
stripping at lockers and   with a towel tied round

leading each other into each other
into the hair and the fold of stomach
and the wet smells of underneath and then
stepping out hot for love or stratagem

I miss my bed   given over for use
by someone else's love   want what's mine
to be just mine   want a world where not all
will get whatever they are looking for

I remember   once   waking and looking
over to the window of my lover
from a room that wasn't his or mine   lost
or something close   the rapture they engage

in   the tipping over
inside and spilling out
lacks happy longing   it's
renewable each night

I go soft from overthinking   we go
back to the cell to have another try
and   hand to your throat   I slowly begin
to build a city never dared before

playing someone else   I throw you down   kiss
from where my hand is gripped to where yours is
I try to be what's expected   but it
dies without reaching to its full extent

and I slump back against the wall   rolled
shoulders   and I don't know if the success
I hear through the wall is real   you stumble
at least in the endeavor we translate

our tongues to speak for us and we just stay there
chest to risen chest   like two beaten wrestlers
who failed their potential   Gunn was right
their skin turns numb   they dress and will depart

this was only ever for a night
there is nothing but the chemical smell
of trying to get clean   the awkward look
the perfect body   lingering on goodbyes

I leave   walk back into early streets
I let the play go on beneath my feet
the night's been drank   the sun is low   the sun
cannot find strength now for another start

CHOKE

isn't this how the best of it should be?
taking the body to the point at which
it almost breaks and then returning
having had your faith restored
in the miraculous fragility
of the self
the night I almost ended us
it was your sobbing brought me back
we talked ourselves together
and   the next day   still wearing your hand
around my neck   I found I was struggling
to swallow   every mouthful
was a labour   I became aware
of the mechanics of my own body
could feel parts of myself that would
usually go unnoticed
after your hand had been on my throat
I learnt the pleasure in possessing
capacities that are never
quite fulfilled   almost being broken
almost leaving but deciding
to tough it out

LEDA TO HER DAUGHTERS

I feel battered

he put the thing his species talks with up inside me
and he talked

daughter   the moment when he opens out and stretches
is when he looks most beautiful

the moment when he looks most beautiful is the moment
right before he breaks your arm

daughter   on his own he's only half a heart

daughter   he made me his pen

he made me do the messy things he keeps
beneath the surface

daughter   his feet

his eyes were hungry for the sky

when he came he made a sound that still hatches
in my throat each morning

how typical of a man

daughter   to pretend he didn't understand

to think my outstretched hand might be an offering of food

daughter   to think that I would feed him

TODAY

you will mistake the gulls
for the screaming of a girl
and run out of your flat
to an empty landing

the wind will come up
from the Mersey   to the satisfaction
of all but the ice cream sellers
huddled around the docks

there will be more people than pavement
people will spend all day singing
other people's songs   and people will throw
coins into the wishingwells of their instrument cases

today   you will break the life of someone
or you'll break yourself apart from them
and   having dressed themselves in you for months
they will be naked and half in shadow as you close the door

today   the light will fall
the breeze will drop   the streets
will empty   the man who stands outside
The Entertainer with the bubble machine

will go home and tell his wife   *it was a bad one*
the wind kept getting under and scattering them
they went everywhere   I lost control   it was like dropping
a bag of marbles in space   it was bedlam

NOT QUITE

each of us having loved each of us
in some earlier room of our lives
there was the awkward intimacy
which only comes from having grasped
between our lips the truest part
of one another   and now the task
of the bedroom   re-hung and altered
pick your euphemistic metaphor
stubbled sandpaper   or the shoulder
crowning weight of lifting a settee
arms we touched seeming to grow towards
our hands as though our hands were light
the mirror   watching ourselves undress

THINGS MEN TAKE

the room above the ceiling
the better pay   the jobs
your space at the bar
the piss   the smell of piss
when they leave a room
the silence   the short road out
and the long road home
the swelling they seem to want
to break the walls with
or they take so much it's easier
to list what it is they leave behind
or they take without asking
like the man who takes the image
of the blond haired girl in the lowcut top
goes home and takes his trousers off
takes the picture of the girl
from the back of his mind
takes his wife in an almost pleasant way
then takes his face over to the wall
takes more than half the duvet
dreams of the short road out
and the long road home
dreams of taking everything
in the house into his hands
dreams his hands are much bigger
than they are

IF IT WASN'T FOR THE NIGHTS

I tour my foreign voice
through the tin roofed halls of semi rural provinces
I barely understand the lines
but the crowd goes mad and claps
of thunder thrum the valley where I sleep
and my lonelyhaircut cellist eyes the bar between us
and I gargle salt   and sleep alone
and back across the border the man I love is curled
to someone else   and they don't speak a word
and   outside   a precious bird doesn't comprehend
the language of its wings
and frost hums on the weathervane

if it wasn't for the nights   Steffan   I'd come home

ii

protest of the physical

I have to bang my hand against some door
to bring myself back to the body

Virginia Woolf

lame arm of the crane   circling
unstocked shelves of half built car park
the day's spent itself already   so early in the evening

  so early in the evening to be spent   to want sleep   to brush
    off our shirts as crumbs the advances of another   too often
    I've said love   tongue to spine   too long spent not touching

a man   alone
a room with a hundred TV screens
                  talk

                            town as talk
        town as a dialogueheavy scene from a Ken Loach film
                 town as a hundred TV screens

the barrelswagger of a man
benched in bandstands with empty
vials of people sitting

                   sleepdeprived and shaking
                    redfaced   drinking
          or already drunk and drinking

people with their songs they stole
from other songs   (town as a borrowed song)
I fought the law and the law aint done yet

                 bus station   the girl
           lights up before she should've
             her top says *call my agent*

birds huddle in the oak trees waiting
for dawn to lift its skirt
clenched fist of the town hall clock

always at 12   arms raised
sun's penetration   surrender
of the day to the streets

graffiti   petrol station wall

this gunna look

               nice

when it's framed

I didn't know it would be the last   love
is giving everything too easily
then staying to try and claw it back

                          nail   spine   pulling at you from inside
                          clothes still on   the verge of undressing
                          and everything we were   was your hoodie

halfway up your body
and my cock half out in your hand
and your *stop it* in a way that meant *don't stop*

                              at least not yet and the swift tug
                          of shirt over head for the soundless spill
                              and the door   your dad

a folk singer is writing
wind catches through the grass like fire
and he's cupping the first bud of a minor classic

                                  town that lost something
                                  town coughing something up
            watching   breathless   as it rolls into a crack in the earth

town on its knees trying to find it
town that shrank into a clenched fist   sweated
on itself   choked one day

                          so that the roads tied up together
                          and people were shouldertoshoulder
                              as in a cage waiting to descend

town that sunk from its centre
like a man winded by a punch
town that bent double   carried

young men   and women   and younger men and women
                          as long as it could but   spinebroken
                                    had to let them go
awake   after waking for what
seemed like hours   the light from the bay
window of the balcony was making rainbows

                                    on the floor   there are days
                          when I don't miss you   or even love you
                                    that much   anymore

something of a naked man and fire
which is prehistoric   which is horrifying
to be undressed so quickly   someone looking on

                                    empty gallery of silence
                                    lines we cannot cross
                          the naked flame   the burning boy

graffiti   Oaks Lane Pithead

pits close
          we still sink
                    into them

Thom   the two opposing wheels of voice
the rough joints of your transatlantic patter
snailing down my neck   undress   love lost

                              room exhausted as an empty city
                                  you're gone   and who alive
                               listens to cassettes anymore?

Thom   you believed your *Touch*
was boring   the wound in the head
healing   skin hardening to the blood

                              undress   touch
                       the only book   blood pumping
                                       Thom   Thom

the fear is to die   untouched   love lost
the smell of ageing   which is really the smell of unclean teeth
to be nowhere   except here   lame arm of the crane   circling

    a memory of gulls   screams from the rollercoaster   two girls
      banging on a door   how thin the membranes that we build
               between each other   how easily broken   opened

qualitative research into pub names in Barnsley
The Mount   The Corner   The Closed Since the Smoking Ban
The Cross Keys   The Bridge   The Soviet   The Station

            The Longbow   The Room   The Glass Half-Full
          The Joseph Bramah   The Keep Drinking   The Mill
                  The White Bear   The We're Still Here

Thom   in boxes   every letter ever wrote
diaries   your fears
of what the love you had might do to him

                            sleep with Thom night after night
                        open at the spine   face pushed deep
                there've been times I've woke and put my arm around

a pillow   halfdreaming it was you   I count what I've got
thinning hair   skin stretched loose from fat
a body only you could love

                            mist frosts across the necks of flats
                            fires smoke themselves irrelevant
                        your most loved song is overplayed

and worn by too many singers
waking to a stomach   hollow   churning   forgetting
all but the briefest inflections of your voice

            your mother called me to the window   fox in the road
                it seemed young   or maybe foxes age more gracefully
                    than us   it was early afternoon   you were sleeping

it seemed lost   wrong place   wrong time
we just watched it burning
down the avenue   red scar

                                    field   way home
                        neighbour with her dog   a man flying
            a model aircraft   just like a real plane   only smaller

graffiti   Barnsley General Hospital

what town of day is it?

is it

          changing?

loves who are lost but are somewhere
everything lost as somewhere
keys to doors of flattened houses

                    intimacy   which means knowing
                          the exact taste of someone else's
                          sleep in their mouth on waking

drunk man to the drunker woman
where you from?   *Barnsley*
Baaaaaaaaaaaaaaaaaarnslie

                        the way people do
          until there are gaps in the tightpacked line of vowels
                that could be rode through   *can tha spell it?*

theory   we've confused happiness
with someone being able to say our name to us
theory   half the people here only know the outside

                    exists because they talk to it through
                    high strung wires while they dream
                    of being recognised on the street

a crowd gathers   some are concerned
a few shout encouragement   most
just want to see what happens when the man jumps

           from the roof of The Queens Hotel   want to see his arms
                grasp the invisible ladder   his elation   his regret
                his body smashed in to infinity on Shambles Street

theory   we're sums of our parts   nerves
nose eyes teeth nails anus spine guts
theory   we're sums of our partners

kissing while trains swim lengths   outside
one platform station   a delay to the thrust of in and out
                    your kiss was deep enough to stand in

days pivot in their sockets so quickly
station   a girl's sudden
flurry of fists   unroosting of doves

                around a young labourer's head   and all journey his face
            is somewhere between a carving and a glass of moving water
                    and his face is covered in paint   its tear stained

I left you because man made fire   then carried
it across the plain   I left you because of peripheral vision
because of crossing oceans   because the moon

                        was only the beginning and there are still places
                                    we haven't marked on maps
                                I left you for a dream in the west

shops on Cheapside open and are closed
in the turn of a month   thunder
the ceaseless roll of the wagon train

                        station   walkhome   man in the doorway
                        of The Mount looking up   *g night luv*
                            theory   the moon isn't just for poets

glimpses of books on trains   C.S. Lewis'
Mere Christianity   *We will be cured of our sin*
at whatever cost to us   *at whatever cost to him*

graffiti   Golden Gate Bridge   San Francisco

this bridge is not

    as beautiful

        as people said

rain   the morning's mundane idea forming
movingloopingringroad of a day
crane's lame arm   same mundane idea

                  the shape
        a fist makes this close to your eye
        and *oh*   *oh*   of beaten door

the small round o   the door   you let him in
the lick   the violence   how the end spits
against the arching   curving   oh

            how much of fighting
        is the need to touch another man?
      you defended me when needed   you were rough

the way you'd clench your teeth in sex
the weeping wrestler   *the weeping wrestler*
your face on the edge of climax

                 lost
      count   invisible numbers   we broke
      the speed of light   2/3rds water   all of us

car parked   edge of a field
murderous night
arm of a justfornow lover

        a voice lights up the quiet zone
          glimpses of articles on trains
      five hours spent shuttling from bed to desk and back again

town as a face with one eye closed
twn as a mspelt txt   town without its eyes
contraction

theory   there is beauty in the ordinary
the row of shops on Shambles Street
the day chasing its own shadow

behind twentythousand windows   threethousand
sexual advances   not all pleasant   not all denied
silent christenings   renaming of each other

a chip shop's neon buzz humps
light into the town   a man
takes a slash in the door

of a train   out west   the restless
bed of the Atlantic   I could have
I should have tried harder

iii

degradation

and now is the time for burning, again
John Riley

HOW TO BE A MAN

SCENE 1

too young to know anything of death

get sent upstairs when someone
knocks at the door on a Sunday

SCENE 2

too young to come back down until you're told   eavesdrop

grandma   are you sure you're OK?
dad   I'm fine

SCENE 3

see your dad's dad dying

the kind of dying where the body forgets itself slowly
how to walk   how to speak   how to swallow solids

SCENE 4

watch your sister hugging the futurefather of her child

go to the other room   computer   television
a comedy impressions show and a joke
about someone's stature
laugh harder than you should have or wanted to

go back to the front room
recount the joke about stature to the seated family

dad   I know   we heard   are you OK?

say you're fine

see your dad's face like an empty box

BACKGROUND CHARACTER NOTES

> you thought you knew how men
> were meant to grieve
> you thought all men felt distant from their fathers
> you thought all men grieved like small Greek women
> in black who say *the bread still needs to be baked*
> you thought men simply carried on
> when your dad unfolded in front of you
> nobody had taught you how to fix him back together

what can you say
is all I can think to say
when the electrician I've met once
working on behalf of a landlord I've never met
calls to say he won't be coming round
because his 18 month old granddaughter is dead

three days earlier he'd texted me
still drunk he said   after his wife's
60th birthday   to ask if he could come
another day   when he learned the baby
wouldn't wake   there might have been a tray of food
still in the room   or a balloon trying to climb the wall

the real horror is him coming to my flat
four days later   silently turning off
the lights and pulling out the switch boxes
that look like intricate rooms in a doll's house
and fitting them back   like that shape game
you give to children when you're trying

to help them make sense of the world

ÓKUNNA ÞÉR RUNNA

translated from the Skaldic poet Egill Skallagrímsson

there are dead in countries
who will never know how
little I despised them
I wanted the penblade
not the bootsplatter trenchlife
the night I ran   there was
sky concealing thunder
a white feather of moon

★

the words give heavy page
the words bleed out of me
bullstrong   I like to think
of guns   the sound of rain
Hemingway's forearm thick
as tree root   men are dead
who never wondered what
I thought   or why   or not

★

I am deadheavydrunk
sharpen penblade   moonglint
now think of Hemingway
swallowing a shotgun
now think of bulls   enraged
now think of men who can't
be men without dying
of rain of Thanes of Harr

MORN

the night is clouding
trees   shadow   nighttrain
Manchester is growing out towards us

the night is raining
fields   go   unrisen
act like you're not waiting

the night is only briefly shining
feralfruit   gloves   empty house
the birthdays of the dead become unseemly

the night is not so much clouding as burying itself

WHEN LOUD THE STORM AND FURIOUS IS THE GALE

the storm has dragged itself offshore
under trees it rains   still

I know a sailor whose mind foamed against itself
and he sat drowning for the next five years

the lighthouse throws its face and catches it
night slicks in over the water

I used to know a shortcut through the dunes
not even dog walkers had spoiled

the shore has dragged itself to sea
the light has the arc of a tethered bird in flight

I have sat in the dune and imagined drowning
in a submarine   heavy death   night slicks

over water it is still raining under trees
I know a shortcut to a sailor   the mind foaming on the beach

THE FACT WE ALMOST KILLED A
BADGER IS INCIDENTAL

what?   the way it flashed its rump to the headlights
at the edge of the carriageway   the way the muscles
churned under the flesh that seemed grey in the dusk
the way you knew it was a badger even though we couldn't
see the markings   the way it missed the wheel by inches

that the near miss   the black and white flight of the beast
into the woods seemed such a moment of freedom
that I went home and ended things with you
don't be ridiculous I'm not superstitious   if we'd tattooed
the road with the fur and the life of it   if we'd flattened it

I still could not have sat through one more night of silence
the fact we almost killed a badger is incidental
anyway   we were going too fast to have stopped

REVELATIONS

every time you fell in love with someone new
you were falling back in love with the first   again
they'd dyed or cut their hair or put on weight
but in the manner of the humble saints who make
the worship of a nameless god relatable   they opened
a window back to the original   when you said their names
it was to call on that first one   to raise what the religious
call a state of grace   so that if there ever was
a reconciliation
their faces would merge into his   and he would be
the love you wept for them
Saint Gavin   Saint Ged   Saint Unknown
of Manchester Bedsit   they were the tangible presence of him
they were the books through which you filled the gaps
that leaving left   the books that were full of their stories
which is your story
which is always the story of a man who left
and the one who must await his return

A GIFT

for the ones I never touched   for the ones
who wanted to watch films   who wanted
to talk   who wanted silence and said I
talked too much   for the one I saw
weeks after   laughing   for the one who served
me coffee and didn't recognise my hands
for the optimistic ones who write

their names on toilet walls   the ones
I never called   for the ones I called
who didn't answer   who left our love
suspended from the ceiling hooks
of that meatmarket city   for the ones
who left and settled down   the ones who wanted
knowledge   were curious   who gained something

from each encounter   used each other
who took what they needed   for everyone
they hurt   who felt burned out   the ones who
didn't realise everyone was burning
the ones who never slept   who died nightly
the ones who said they'd kill for it   for all of them
a gift   we were young   we only had our bodies

FINALLY

a day will come   when
woken by the xylophone
of sunthroughblinds
you'll realise

that the beach was not the place
where horses tore the sand
to ribbon

that the scent of him has lifted
from the last of the sheets
that he isn't coming back

that it hasn't rained
but the birds are pretending that it has
so they can sing

NOTES & ACKNOWLEDGEMENTS

'Jacob with the angel' is for Okey

'not quite' is for Andy and Matt

'protest of the physical' is for Steffan

'the fact we almost killed a badger is incidental' is for Liz

'the schoolboys' has   in its background   the celebrations held in some South Yorkshire villages after the death of Margaret Thatcher

'Saturday night' takes each fourth line from Thom Gunn's 'Saturday Night'

'Leda to her daughters' was first inspired by Paul Delaux's painting 'Leda'

'ókunna þér runna' was written as part of the Viking Poets project thanks to Debbie Potts for getting me involved

'Jacob with the angel' won first prize in the 2012 Live Canon Poetry Competition

'Protest of the Physical' was first published as a pamphlet by Red Squirrel Press   thanks to Sheila Wakefield for all her support over the years

thanks to New Writing North whose award of a substantial Northern Writers' Award helped with the writing of this book thanks also to Carol Gorner and the Gordon Burn Trust for the kind use of the cottage where this collection was finished

thanks to Robin Robertson for all his editorial input and support

thanks to Sean Hewitt   Sarah Hymas   Kim Moore   Helen Mort
Okey Nzelu   David Tait   Thomas Stewart   Alicia Stubbersfield
and all the others who provided invaluable help with these poems

thanks to the editors of the following magazines and anthologies in
which earlier versions of some of these poems appeared   *Astronaut
Cast: The Poetry Business Book of New Contemporary Poets   Eyewear
In the Red   London Review of Books   Magma   Modern Poetry in
Translation   Oxford Poetry   Poem   Sculpted: Poetry of the North West
Shearsman   The Best British Poetry 2013   The Rialto*

thanks to Steffan and Gerard   with all my love   for letting me
write what we had